HAL•LEONARD
INSTRUMENTAL PLAY-ALONG

AUDIO ACCESS INCLUDED

PLAYBACK+
Speed • Pitch • Balance • Loop

VIOLA

IRISH FAVORITES

CONTENTS

To access audio visit:
www.halleonard.com/mylibrary

Enter Code
2125-0692-9890-1543

ISBN 978-1-4234-9532-1

HAL•LEONARD®

Visit Hal Leonard Online at
www.halleonard.com

Contact us:
Hal Leonard
7777 West Bluemound Road
Milwaukee, WI 53213
Email: info@halleonard.com

In Europe, contact:
Hal Leonard Europe Limited
42 Wigmore Street
Marylebone, London, W1U 2RN
Email: info@halleonardeurope.com

In Australia, contact:
Hal Leonard Australia Pty. Ltd.
4 Lentara Court
Cheltenham, Victoria, 3192 Australia
Email: info@halleonard.com.au

BELIEVE ME, IF ALL THOSE
ENDEARING YOUNG CHARMS

VIOLA

Words and Music by
THOMAS MOORE

THE BELLS OF ST. MARY'S

VIOLA

Words by DOUGLAS FURBER
Music by A. EMMETT ADAMS

BLACK VELVET BAND

VIOLA

Traditional

BRENNAN ON THE MOOR

VIOLA

Traditional

COCKLES AND MUSSELS
(Molly Malone)

VIOLA

Traditional

THE CROPPY BOY

VIOLA

18th Century Irish Folksong

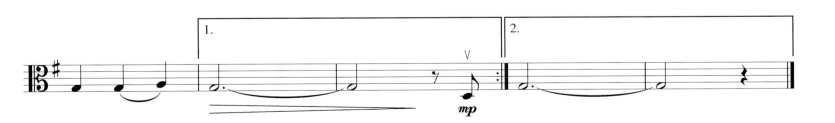

DANNY BOY

VIOLA

Words by FREDERICK EDWARD WEATHERLY
Traditional Irish Folk Melody

EASY AND SLOW

VIOLA

Traditional

THE FOGGY DEW

VIOLA

Traditional

GREEN GROW THE RUSHES, O

VIOLA

Traditional

THE HUMOUR IS ON ME NOW

VIOLA

Traditional

I ONCE LOVED A LASS

VIOLA

Traditional

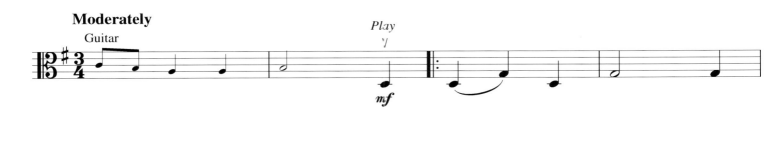

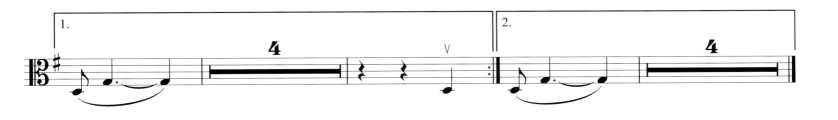

I'LL TAKE YOU HOME AGAIN, KATHLEEN

VIOLA

Words and Music by
THOMAS WESTENDORF

I'LL TELL ME MA

VIOLA

Traditional

THE IRISH ROVER

VIOLA

Traditional

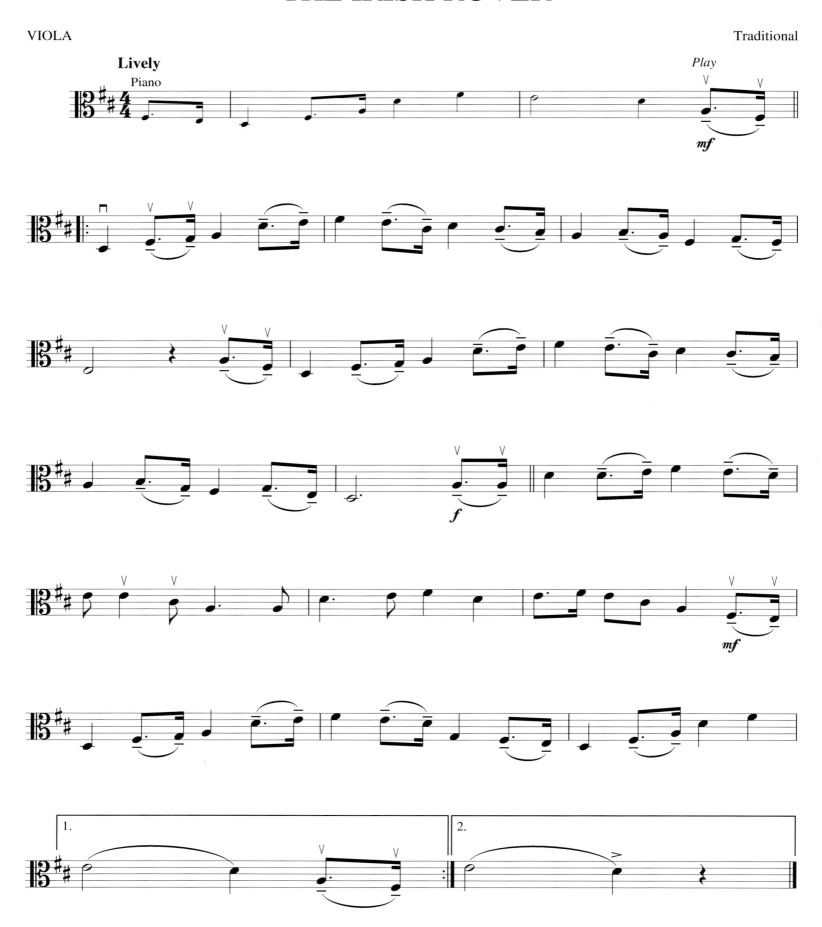

THE JOLLY BEGGARMAN

VIOLA

Traditional

THE LITTLE BEGGARMAN

VIOLA

Traditional

MacNAMARA'S BAND

Words by JOHN J. STAMFORD
Music by SHAMUS O'CONNOR

VIOLA

MINSTREL BOY

VIOLA

Traditional

MY WILD IRISH ROSE

VIOLA

Words and Music by
CHAUNCEY OLCOTT

A NATION ONCE AGAIN

VIOLA

Words and Music by
THOMAS DAVIS

THE OLD ORANGE FLUTE

VIOLA

Traditional

THE PATRIOT GAME

VIOLA

Traditional

RED IS THE ROSE

VIOLA

Irish Folksong

THE RISING OF THE MOON

VIOLA

Traditional

THE ROSE OF TRALEE

VIOLA

Words by C. MORDAUNT SPENCER
Music by CHARLES W. GLOVER

TOO-RA-LOO-RA-LOO-RAL
(That's an Irish Lullabye)

Words and Music by
JAMES R. SHANNON

VIOLA

THE WEARING OF THE GREEN

VIOLA

18th Century Irish Folksong

WHEN IRISH EYES ARE SMILING

VIOLA

Words by CHAUNCEY OLCOTT
and GEORGE GRAFF, JR.
Music by ERNEST R. BALL

THE WILD COLONIAL BOY

VIOLA

Traditional

WILD ROVER

VIOLA

Traditional